Ferdinand Courtney French

The Concept of Law in Ethics

Ferdinand Courtney French

The Concept of Law in Ethics

ISBN/EAN: 9783337232566

Printed in Europe, USA, Canada, Australia, Japan

Cover: Foto ©Suzi / pixelio.de

More available books at **www.hansebooks.com**

THE

CONCEPT OF LAW IN ETHICS.

THESIS ACCEPTED BY THE FACULTY OF CORNELL UNIVERSITY
FOR THE PH. D. DEGREE IN PHILOSOPHY.

BY

COURTNEY FRENCH, A. B. (Brown)

School of Philosophy of Cornell University.

VIDENCE, R. I.

ON & ROUNDS.

1892.

EX LIBRIS

THE

CONCEPT OF LAW IN ETHICS.

THESIS ACCEPTED BY THE FACULTY OF CORNELL UNIVERSITY
FOR THE PH. D. DEGREE IN PHILOSOPHY.

―――――――

BY

FERDINAND COURTNEY FRENCH, A. B. (BROWN)

Fellow in the Sage School of Philosophy of Cornell University.

PROVIDENCE, R. I.

PRESTON & ROUNDS.

1892.

Nur das Gesetz kann uns die Freiheit geben.

Goethe.

πλήρωμα οὖν νόμου ἡ ἀγάπη.

Romans xiii., 10.

CONTENTS.

CHAPTER I.

Jural Aspects of Ancient Ethics.

CHAPTER II.

Christian and Mediæval Ethics.

CHAPTER III.

Modern Ethics.

CHAPTER IV.

The Moral Law.

CHAPTER I.

§ 1. A law, in the primary sense of the term, is a rule of human action prescribed by authority. The use of this term to express the order of nature is a derived one which became current only after considerable historical development.[1] Even this first-mentioned usage is primary only in a relative sense. At the dawn of history we find men ruled by custom rather than law. Clans, tribes and village communities were ruled by institutions which mythology might explain as established by the gods, or by the ancestors of the race, but in either case for the living generation they were a fixed body of rules that could not be infringed without incurring on the individual and on the community the severe displeasure of the gods, and which men regarded as no more subject to change on their part than the paths of the sun, moon and stars. History opens with this reign of custom, but it must have been only by a long evolution in prehistoric times that this 'cake of custom' was established. In the struggle for existence among primitive men nothing could have been of more importance than organization.[2] The elimination of unorganized groups by their better organized contemporaries must have brought about the survival of those customs and common norms of conduct which served to unify each group into an organic body. It was of little matter whether these customs were such as we should call good or bad, provided only they brought the individual into subordination to the community, and en-

1 So. Holland, *Elements of Jurisprudence*, p. 15, and Zeller, *Ueber Begriff und Begründung der Sittlichen Gesetze, Vorträge u. Abhandnngen, Samml*, p. 189. Max Müller points out a possible exception to this in the Sanskrit *Rita*, which he explains as meaning originally the order of nature and afterwards being applied to the moral order.

2 Bagehot, *Physics and Politics*.

abled the latter to stand together as a unit against all foes from without. We have, perhaps, an illustration of the prehistoric state of society in the description of the Cyclops in the Odyssey, a description that may well have been suggested to the poet by the mode of life among some alien and less advanced people : [1]

"They have neither assemblies for consultation nor judicial decrees, . . . but every one exercises jurisdiction over his children and wives, and they pay no regard to one another."[2]

But whatever may have been the course of this prehistoric evolution of institutions and ideas, the earliest historic prototype of law is custom. Or, if we may extend the term to this pre-natal state of the concept, we may say that customary law was the progenitor of positive law.[3] The etymology of the word law, "that which lies or is fixed or set," [4] and of similar words in other languages, points back to the time when laws were the established norms of immemorial custom rather than the commands of a sovereign authority. The head of the tribe, or the village council, in administering justice, were regarded as possessing only a judicial and never a legislative function.[5]

Among primitive peoples we find no distinction made between laws of the state, requirements of religious ritual, and the demands of morality. Conduct in all these respects was governed by an undifferentiated mass of rules, which were enforced upon the individual, not only by the severest human penalties, but by the even more terrible fears of superhuman powers. Little real force, however, is required to secure obedience to customary law. The immobility of habit, public opinion, and superstition, all combine to make disobedience well nigh impossible.

1 Maine, *Ancient Law*, p. 125.

2 *Odyssey* ix., 114.

3 Maine, *Early History of Institutions.* Lect. xiii.

4 Century Dictionary.

5 Maine, *Ancient Law*—"It is certain that in the infancy of mankind, no sort of legislature, not even a distinct author of law is contemplated or conceived of. Law has scarcely reached the footing of custom ; it is rather a habit." p. 8.

"There is no system of recorded law literally from China to Peru," says Sir Henry Maine, "which, when it first emerges into notice, is not seen to be entangled with religious ritual and observance." [1]

The general conclusion thus expressed by Maine as the result of his studies of institutions in India, is equally true of the early Greeks. This primitive confusion of law, religion and morality among the Greeks is well described in the following passage from Grote:

⎛ "In historical Athens the great impersonal authority called 'The Laws,' stood out separately, both as guide and sanction, distinct from religious duty or private sympathies; but of this discriminated conception of positive law and positive morality the germ only can be detected in the Homeric poems. The appropriate Greek word for human laws never occurs. Amidst a very wavering phraseology we can detect a gradual transition from the primitive idea of a personal goddess Themis, attached to Zeus, first to his sentences or orders called Themistes, and next by a still farther remove to various established customs, which these sentences were believed to sanctify—the authority of religion and that of custom coalescing into one indivisible obligation." [2] ⎠

The word $\nu\acute{o}\mu o\varsigma$, denoting etymologically "that which is assigned or appointed," [3] is the proper Greek term for law. This is the first word to acquire and retain anything like the meaning which we now express by law. The Romans translated $\nu\acute{o}\mu o\varsigma$ by *lex* and then carried over into Latin and handed down to modern nations the conception which the Greeks had acquired and embalmed in the word. The English word has derived its meaning not so much from etymology and early Teutonic uses, as from the combined influence of Greek, Latin and Hebrew terms which it has been used to translate. In tracing the development of the Greek concept of $\nu\acute{o}\mu o\varsigma$, therefore, we are studying the early history of our own concept of law. This word was not used by Homer. It is found first in Hesiod. At Athens $\nu\acute{o}\mu o\varsigma$ was the name given especially to

1 Maine, *Early Law and Custom.* Chap. 1.
2 Grote, *History of Greece*, vol. ii., p. 110.
3 Liddell & Scott, Lexicon.

the laws of Solon (those of Draco being called *θεσμοί*) and then generally to laws, ordinances, particularly to fundamental laws in distinction from *ψήφισμα* special bills, or decrees.[1]

§ 2. 'Since in early times legal and moral ideas were indiscriminately combined under the general notion of customary law, we must look for the beginning of the history of the concept of law in morality, where the tendency to discriminate between the two fields of conduct first manifests itself. It is not a case of a concept developed in one sphere of life and then carried over by analogy or metaphor to another; it is rather a case of differentiation. We do not find moral and legal institutions existing side by side and then after a time the notions developed in one sphere transferred to the other. Rather is conduct as a whole ruled by one homogeneous mass of customs. The first beginning of the distinction between moral and civil law is seen in the division of custom or law into *written* and *unwritten*. The written law, being the expressed will of the king or state, enforced by penalties, corresponds to our notion of law in the jural sense, while the unwritten law, which depended for its binding force on habit, public opinion, religious belief and conscience, answers in a general way to our notion of moral law. The unwritten law was regarded as the foundation and source of the written. The latter only is changeable, the former is original and abiding. This division of the law is very common in Greek literature.[2] One of the earliest and most famous examples of this is in Sophocles. Antigone defies the king, who has forbidden her to bury her brother in these words:

> " Nor did I deem thy edicts strong enough,
> That thou, a mortal man, should'st over-pass
> The unwritten laws of God that know not change.
> They are not of to-day nor yesterday,
> But live forever, nor can man assign
> When first they sprang to being." [3]

Aristotle classifies laws as peculiar and universal—peculiar laws being such as have been marked out by each people in

1 Lexicon.
2 Schmidt, *Die Ethik der Alten Griechen*, p. 201.
3 Sophocles, *Antigone*, l. 450, (Plumptre's translation.)

reference to itself, and being partly written and partly un-written—universal laws being those which are conformable merely to the dictates of nature. "For there does exist naturally one universal sense of right and wrong, which in a certain degree all intuitively divine even should no inter-course with each other, nor any compact have existed."[1] In this connection Aristotle cites Empedodes as saying of a cer-tain maxim "that it is not right here and wrong there, but a principle of law to all. It is extended uninterruptedly throughout the spacious firmament and boundless light." Another term for the unwritten law is equity which has to do with the intention of the lawgiver rather than the lan-guage of the law, and with the whole tenor and principle of the agent's conduct rather than with specific acts.[2] Equity may controvene the written law. In the Ethics he says of the nature of the equitable, that it is a correction of law when-ever the law is defective owing to its generality.[3] Again he says of equity that it "remains forever and varies not at any time, neither does the universal law, for this is in conformity to nature, but the written law does frequently vary."[4]

The reduction of a portion of the ancient customs to writing and the notion thus introduced of a written law in contrast with the unwritten law, must have been one of the first steps toward the development of the concept of posi-tive law. But even the written law differs essentially from our modern notion of enacted law. It was not looked upon as the recorded will of an established legislative authority, but rather as a written precipitate of ancestral customs. Plato and Aristotle regarded the distinction between law and cus-tom as quite unessential.[5]

§ 3. Another influence in developing the notion of posi-itive law was the contrast which the Sophists, and later the Cynics,[6] made between *law* and *nature*.[7] The Sophists were

1 Aristotle, *Rhetoric*, I., xiii., 2, (Browne's tranlation.)
2 *Rhetoric*, I., xiii., 17.
3 *Ethics*, v. 10.
4 *Rhetoric*, I., xv.
5 Schmidt, *Die Ethik der Alten Griechen*, p. 202.
6 Zeller, *Socrates and the Socratic Schools*, p. 322.
7 νόμος and φύσις.

the individualists and iconoclasts of custom in the fifth century. Hippias is represented in Xenophon as "disputing the moral obligation of laws because they so often change, while he acknowledges as divine or natural law only that which is everywhere equally observed.   In Plato he says that law, like a tyrant, compels men to do much that is contrary to nature." [1]

This opposition of law to nature must have made much more definite in men's minds, than ever before, the notion of a positive law dependent upon the will of men. It brought out the distinction between legislation as a voluntary act, creative of law, and the mere formulation of already existing customs. Some of the Sophists went so far as to declare all positive law to be arbitrary enactments set up by those in power for their own advantage, and as laws and usage had been regarded hitherto as the only moral authority, this doctrism seemed to dissolve at once all moral as well as political obligation. The distinction between written and unwritten, and the opposition of law to nature combined to develop and make definite the notion of law as the enacted will of rational beings.

§ 4. With Stoicism another idea came into prominence, the idea of *natural law* or the *law of nature*. In the Greek conception of natural law we have something quite different from the natural laws of modern science. We find here the universal, unwritten norms of conduct and the order of physical phenomena combined under the single notion of law of nature. Laws which prevailed among all nations and were acknowledged as binding by all peoples, such as the sanctity of oaths, the duty of hospitality, etc., could not, it was evident, have been founded by any prince, or city, or revealed by the divinities or oracles of any particular people; they must have their source in the universal divine will and be revealed by nature to all men in their own consciousness.[2] Such universal and unwritten laws as norms of human conduct, we have already seen, were widely recognized by the

1 Zeller, *Pre-Socratic Philosophy.* Vol. ii., p. 476.
2 Zeller, *Ueber Begriff und Begründung der Sittlichen Gesetze*, p. 190.

Greeks. Heracleitus was, perhaps, the first to connect expressly this divine law with the order of things in the physical world.[1] Often the two were set in opposition, and even those who insisted most emphatically on the invariable necessity of the natural order as, e. g, Empedodes, Plato, and Aristotle, did not designate this by the term law.[2] With very few exceptions before the time of the Stoics this word was applied exclusively to norms of human conduct, the laws of nature, when this expression was used, meaning such rules of conduct as were common to all men and binding upon them by virtue of their very nature.

"It was the founder of the Stoic school," says Zeller, "who first brought into common use the concept of law as applied to the natural order of things."[3] The extension of law from the sphere of human action to the physical world was a natural consequence of the fundamental doctrines of Stoicism. The Stoics believed in an ultimate ground and cause of the world which was not merely the material substance of things, but was at the same time the creative Reason. The natural order and necessity in the universe they regarded as the expression of the will of that Ultimate Reason and hence called it the law of nature. As man and nature are both under the same divine lawgiver, no distinction was made between natural law and moral law.[4] In the absence of scientific precision the same confusion prevailed throughout the Middle Ages. The laws that determine the

---

1 Zeller, *Pre-Socratic Philosophy*, p. 41. An early example of the concept of law in its broadest aspect is the saying of Pindar:

> Νόμος, ὁ πάντων βασιλεὺς
> θνατῶν τε καὶ ἀθανάτων.

2 Zeller, *Ueber Begriff*, etc. Plato in the Trimaeus 83 E seems to use the phrase 'laws of nature' in something like the modern scientific sense. Zeller finds one such case in Aristotle, see essay *Ueber Begriff*, etc., note 11.

3 Ibid. p. 192.

4 Chrysippus, according to Diog. Laert., vii. 88, calls the "common law right reason which pervades all things, being identical with Zeus, the ruler of the government of the universe."

νόμος was frequently called by the Stoics λόγος ὀρθός, and Cicero says Lex vera ratio est recta summi Jovis.—*De legibus*, ii. 4. For further examples see Zeller, *Stoics, Epicureans and Sceptics*, p. 241, note.

order of nature and those which express the duty of man were regarded alike as divine commands. It is only since the sixteenth and seventeenth centuries that philosophers and men of science have held a clear conception of natural law as the expression of the uniformities of the phenomenal world, in distinction from the primary use of law as applied to norms of human conduct.

§ 5.   Were we tracing the history of the concept of law in physical science, we should have now to consider what use the Stoics made of this law of nature in explaining the material world.   Our interest here, however, is in the use they made of the concept in their moral philosophy.

The central problem of Greek ethics was not to determine the moral laws, but rather to find the chief good and the mode of conduct which would secure it.   It was the doctrine of goods, rather than the doctrine of duties which gave the key-note to the whole moral philosophy of the Greeks.   With the Stoics, as with their contemporaries and opponents, the Epicureans, and with Aristotle before them, the aim is to determine the highest good of life.[1]   The Epicureans pronounced pleasure the highest good ; the Stoics, virtue,[2] and virtue they explained as conduct according to the laws of nature.[3]   These laws of nature are not conceived so much as imperatives of the divine will which ought to be obeyed because thus commanded, but rather as ordinances of the divine reason, compliances with which can alone secure weal to rational beings.

The fundamental being of the universe was described by the Stoics by a variety of terms, all meaning the same, one primary force permeating the whole world—God, Soul of the World, Providence, Destiny, Reason of the World, Universal Law, Nature.[4]   The good in every system of thought must be based on the general arrangement of the world, and as the Stoics understood the world to be a cosmos governed by Reason, they consequently found the good of the indi-

1 Zeller, *Stoics, Epicureans and Sceptics*, p. 225.
2 Ibid. p. 229.
3 Ibid. p. 254.
4 Ibid. p. 148 ff.

vidual in submitting himself to the laws of this universal reason.   Obedience is not imposed upon men by authority
from without, but men are bound by their very desire for the
highest good to obey the laws of their own rational nature,
which are at the same time the laws of the rational universe.
The grand principle of human life, then, is to live according
to nature.   But by nature the Stoics meant almost the oppo-
site of what is ordinarily meant by that term.   To follow
nature with them is not to give loose rein to one's native
passions and emotions ; it is to conform to the universal and
rational.[2]   Emotions and passions they regarded as a product
of the irrational elements[3] in our make-up and as such to be
neglected by the wise men.   Hence the modern usage of the
term "Stoical."   This failure to provide for the legitimate ex-
ercise of the emotions is the prominent defect in the Stoic
theory of morals—a consequence which followed quite easily
from their too exclusively rational interpretation of nature.
An adequate ethics will find scope for all of man's faculties
and powers, for the symmetrical development of all sides of
his nature.

The Stoics denounced existing customs and preached the
doctrine of nature, but it was the rational, not the emotional
nature, and it was the nature of the future, and not the nature of the past.   They did not look for improvement in a re-
turn to some golden age of innocence, but in a progressive
moral culture of men according to the laws of the rational
nature.   They set before themselves the type of a perfect
wise man, a type which they admitted no one had yet realized
in himself, but which was to them, nevertheless, the ideal
goal of moral effect.   "Zeno and the rest, though they do
not claim to be wise, yet claimed to be 'advancing.'   This notion of conscious moral progress and self discipline is too
familiar now for us easily to believe that it was first introduced into Greece in the third century B. C.   It may be said,

---

1 Ibid. p. 240.

2 Grant, *The Ethics of Aristotle*, Vol. I., Essay vi.   *The Ancient Stoics*,
p. 319.

3 " Emotion or passion is a movement of mind contrary to reason and
nature." Zeller, *Stoics*, etc., p. 244.

indeed, to be contained implicitly in Aristotle's theory of
'habits,' but it is in reality the expression of a new and
totally different spirit. By this spirit we shall find the later
Stoics deeply penetrated. It constituted perhaps the most
purely 'moral' notion of antiquity, as implying the deepest
associations, which are attached to the word moral." [1]

Closely connected with the modern concept of moral law
is the idea of duty. Though quite in harmony with their general mode of thought and intense moral earnestness, the notion of duty as a distinct moral concept does not seem to
have been grasped by the Greek Stoics.[2] In the term
καθῆκον, 'the suitable,' 'the fitting,' 'the proper,' we have
the 'lineal antecedent' of our duty. This is the term
which was translated into Latin by *officium*. It was probably
under the influences of the Roman sternness of character
and reverence for law that this notion of duty as the correlate
of law first came to consciousness.[3]

The Stoics exalted the individual in contrast with the institutions and laws of human states, but only to subordinate him
again to the universal Reason and the laws of the cosmic
state. The cosmopolitanism of the Stoics was an integral
part of their moral philosophy. It was a cosmopolitanism,
too, in the broadest etymological sense of the term ; [4] it not
only brought the individual into a common citizenship and
brotherhood of all nations, but also made him as a rational being a partaker of the rational life of the whole cosmos.
The universe is one city governed by the one law of nature
and hence all rational beings, as subjects of this law, must
be fellow-citizens of the one world-city.[5] The fact that the
founders of the Stoic school were men of foreign birth[6] who

1 Grant, *Ethics of Aristotle.* Vol. I., p 324.

2 " Und so fehlt denn der Begriff der Pflicht den Systemen der Griechen
völlig." Ziegler, *Die Ethik der Griechen und Romer*, p. 241.

3 Grant, *The Ethics of Aristotle.* Vol. I., Essay vi., p. 325.

4 Ibid. p. 326.

5 Zeller, *Stoics*, etc., p. 326. " Reason is the common law for all, and
those who owe allegiance to one law are members of one state." p. 330.

6 Zeller says (*Stoics*, etc., p. 36) : " Nearly all the most important Stoics before the Christian era belong by birth to Asia Minor, to Syria, and
to the islands of the Eastern Archipelago." Grant gives a list of the

came to Greece in adult life, was doubtless influential in en-
abling them to transcend the limitations of Hellenic institutions. The conquests of Alexander, too, had broadened
Greek knowledge of the barbarians and made it possible for
the thinkers of the third century to realize the common
humanity in all peoples as it had never been possible before.
But while the foreign birth of the early Stoics may have
made it easier for them to deduce the cosmopolitan conclusions of their system, and the Macedonian conquests may
have made their hearers more accessible to such views, yet
despite all the influences of these two concurrent circumstances, we must regard the cosmopolitanism of the Stoics
as a necessary consequence of their fundamental conception
of the universe as rational, and all men as subject to the law
of universal reason.   Plato had sunk the individual in the
state.   The Sophists regarded men as lawless atoms, essentially unrelated.   By the doctrine of the Universal Reason
and the law of nature the Stoics escaped both of these ex-
tremes.   While doing full justice to the individual, they still
emphasized his subordination to law and order.

Due weight had been given to the moral significance of
the state and legal institutions in the earlier systems,[1] but
the Stoics were the first to take the term law out of its
strictly jural sense and apply it in a wider and more distinct-
tively moral field.   The deep ethical import of law is perhaps nowhere more clearly manifested than in the famous
hymn of Cleanthes to Zeus: "Thou makest order out of
disorder, and what is worthless becomes precious in thy
sight; for thou hast fitted together good and evil into one
and hast established one law, that exists forever.   But the

early Stoics and their places of birth (*Ethics of Aristotle*, Vol. I; p. 308),
and advances the theory that the peculiar moral earnestness of the Stoic
philosophy was of Semitic origin and 'alien from the childlike and
unconscious spirit of the Hellenic mind, with its tendency to objective
thought and the enjoyment of nature.'

[1] Schmidt *Die Ethik der Alten Griechen*, p. 198.   "Euripides refers
the distinction of right and wrong to the laws.   Kallicles in the Gorgias
(482 e–483 c) designates the content of morality as that which corresponds
to the law and so takes law and morality as meaning the same."   Ibid.
p. 200.

wicked fly from thy law, unhappy ones, and though they desire to possess what is good, yet they see not, neither do they hear, the universal law of God. . . . O Zeus, giver of all things, who dwellest in dark clouds, and rulest over the thunder, deliver men from their foolishness. Scatter it from their souls, and grant them to obtain wisdom, for by wisdom thou dost rightly govern all things ; that being honored we may repay thee with honour, singing thy works without ceasing, as is right for us to do. For there is no greater thing than this, either for mortal men or for the gods, to sing rightly the universal law." [1]

§ 6. The notion of law thus borrowed from jurisprudence was destined to be returned with interest. The most signal triumph of the Stoic doctrine of natural law was on the field of Roman law. Ziegler says of the philosophy of the Stoa that it "is of the greatest significance for the history of Ethics not only on its own account, but also above all, because it entered the Roman world as a ferment and exercised there in troubled times a mighty influence on the best minds theoretically and practically." [2] The conception of a law of nature furnished the statesmen and jurists of Rome with a moral basis for their law and an ideal by which to direct its reformation and development. [3] No other idea of Greek philosophy found such a keen appreciation at Rome or exercised anything like as great an influence on Roman thought. The Romans had no taste for metaphysics and Greek speculations in general excited only a dilettante interest among them.

Two kinds of law were early recognized at Rome. At the the time when Greek philosophic thought began to be felt among the Romans these two bodies of law had been developing for centuries not entirely without influence on one an-

1 This hymn is preserved by Stobæus, *Ecl. Phys.*, I, 30. The Greek is given by Ueberweg, *History of Philosophy*, Vol. I., p. 197. The selection quoted is from the rendering of Grant, *Ethics of Aristotle*, Vol. I, p. 329.

2 Ziegler, *Die Ethik der Griechen und Römer*, p. 165.

3 For the influence of Stoicism on Roman Law see Grant, *Ethics of Aristotle*, Vol. I., p. 340, ff; Morey, *Outlines of Roman Law*, p. 107, ff; Maine, *Ancient Law*, Chap III., ' Law of Nature and Equity.'

other, but yet each by itself and along its own path. The civil law (*jus civile*) was the law of the Roman citizen. It owed its origin to the religious conception of the early Romans[1] and was regarded as binding upon and applicable to such only as participated in the religion of the city. This law was first put in writing in the former Twelve Tables. The presence of foreigners in the city and the needs of commerce early showed the necessity of a law applicable to those who were not citizens. Since strangers could not be judged by the sacred civil law of Rome, the Praetor to whose court such cases were brought sought out and applied the various legal principles common to the surrounding Italian tribes. It was the custom for the Praetor each year, on beginning his term of office, to publish an edict setting forth the principles on which he proposed to adjudicate the cases brought before him. Each new Praetor published the edict of his predecessor, making such additions as he deemed advisable. As this body of law was established to judge foreigners by, and was supposed to consist of laws common to all the tribes and nationalities represented at Rome, it was called the *jus gentium* or Law of Nations. Constructed thus from principles common to a number of tribes, the *jus gentium* was much less cumbered by legal technicalities and formulas and was much more liberal and equitable than the *jus civile*. In spite of the contempt which the Romans had for it as the law of foreigners it still exercised a humanizing influence over the civil law itself.

From the middle of the second century B. C. on, Greek philosophy was studied by the leading minds at Rome. Epicureanism helped to break down the superstitious fears of the old gods, but its ethics met with no marked response. The ethics of Stoicism, however, appealed to the moral sense of the nation. Law took on a new and profoundly ethical aspect. Its ultimate seat and authority was seen to be not

1 "This religion had produced laws; the relations among men—property, inheritance, legal proceedings—all were regulated not by the principles of natural equity, but by the dogmas of this religion, and with a view to the requirements of its worship." De Coulanges, *The Ancient City*, p. 519.

in the founder of the city or in the will of changeable deities, but in the unchangeable nature of things. As the Romans compared their actual laws with the Stoic ideal of natural law, they saw that the despised *jus gentium* came much nearer to that ideal than their revered *jus civile*. It possessed in a far higher degree those marks of simplicity and harmony which have always been regarded as characterizing the works of nature. The old feeling of contempt for the *jus gentium* gradually gave way and the Roman Jurists brought up under Stoic teachings came to look upon it with reverence as a partial embodiment, or perhaps as a remnant of that ancient law of nature. No one contributed more to this change of sentiment than Cicero. 'The first important attempt made by the Roman writers to ground law upon nature we find in the ' Laws ' of Cicero where the fundamental proposition is laid down that man is born for justice and that law and equity are not a mere establishment of opinion, but are an institution of nature.'[1]

Legal development and reform under the Republic had been empirical, unconscious, so to speak, the result of procedure. Under the Empire, however, guided and stimulated by the ideal of natural law, progress was conscious and rapid. The old civil law became more and more circumscribed and one after another of its formalities was abandoned. 'The preference accorded by jurists and judges to the *jus gentium* over the *jus civile* is insufficient to account for these and many other changes in the same direction, as well as for the ever increasing tendency evinced to subordinate word and deed to the *voluntas* (intention) from which they arose. They are rather to be attributed to the striving on the part of many after a higher ideal, to which they gave the name of *jus naturale*.'[2] Among the intensely practical Romans this ideal of law worked a reformatory and never a revolutionary influence, as has been the case in modern times. 'The value and serviceableness of the conception arose from its keeping before the mental vision a type of perfect law and

---

1 Morey, *Outlines of Roman Law.*
2 Muirhead, *Law of Rome*, p. 297

from its inspiring the hope of an indefinite approximation to it, at the same time that it never tempted the practitioner or the citizen to deny the obligation of existing laws which had not been adjusted to the theory. . . . I know no reason why the law of the Romans should be superior to the laws of the Hindoos, unless the theory of Natural Law had given it a type of excellence different from the usual one. In this one exceptional instance, simplicity and symmetry were kept before the eyes of society whose influence on mankind was destined to be prodigious from other causes, as the charac-teristic of an ideal and absolutely perfect law.'[1]

The laws of Rome as finally formulated by the great jurists and handed down to posterity was the happy union of Roman practice and Greek theory. The Stoic notion of natural law furnished an ideal and ethical basis for the practical legal institution of Rome, and in so doing gave them a breadth and depth of meaning that has made them of incalculable value for all time.[2] In the code of Justinian the theory of law of nature was preserved through the Middle Ages. Un-der the influence of the Church and of the Romanized cities the old law as a body of practical rules was kept in use by the Germanic conquerors even in the darkest ages. Scien-tific study of the law and its principles, however, was sus-pended and not revived till about the beginning of the twelfth century. It was then that the University of Bologna be-came famous as a seat of legal studies, and never since has the law of Rome ceased to be studied in the principal insti-tutions of learning in Western Europe.

It would be a most interesting historical study to go on from this point and trace the influence of the Stoic doctrine of law of nature embodied and preserved as it was in Ro-man law ;[3] to show how this doctrine effected the develop-

---

1 Maine, *Ancient Law*, p. 76, 78.

2 (Roman Law) " endures still, furnishing the spirit, principles, and to a great extent the substance of all modern bodies of law, second in for-warding civilization to no single force save Christianity." Andrews, *In-stitutes of General History*, p. 78.

3 Maine, *Ancient Law*, Chap. IV. 'The Modern History of the Law of Nature.' "The importance of this theory to mankind has been much greater that its philosophical deficiencies would lead us to expect." p. 74.

ment of jurisprudence in France ; how the alliance with the
lawyers enabled the king to solidify and centralize the mon-
archy ; how, later, Rousseau made of this jural doctrine a
political doctrine, which thus became the watchword of the
French Revolution ;[1] how the same doctrine gave a theoretic basis to the men who carried through the English Revolution, and how again the same thought learned from Locke,
Montesquieu and Rousseau animated the American Revolution.   We must not turn aside, however, to follow this notion
of natural law through the tangled web of jurisprudence,
theories of the state, and practical politics.   Our purpose here
is to trace the notion of law in the principal systems of ethics
noticing the ethical ideas in jurisprudence and politics only
so far as they have had a reflex influence on moral philosophy.

[1] Ibid. p. 80: "The theory of Natural Law is the source of most all
the special ideas as to law, politics and society which France, during the
last hundred years has been the instrument of diffusing all over the
western world."

CHAPTER II.

§ 7. In the Middle Ages morals and religion, ethics and theology, were inextricably confounded. Nor could we expect it to have been otherwise. Classical culture had gone out and the only intellectual life of the times was in the Church. Philosophy was the handmaid of theology. It is, therefore, in the works of the Christian theologians that we must look for a continuation of the stream of ethical thought. Remembering the stern denunciation which the founder of Christianity pronounced against the legalism of the Scribes and Pharisees, and his constant insistance upon 'inwardness' i. e., a rectitude of heart and spirit and a positive good-will (ἡ ἀγάπη), we might expect to find the notion of law playing but a small part in Christian Ethics. Three facts may be mentioned whose influence on Christianity combined to give a jural form to its moral teachings :

1. The Hebrew origin of Christianity.

As among all early peoples, so in the case of the Israelites, religion, morality and civil law were presented to the popular consciousness in one undifferentiated mass of rules. The law of Moses, the code of ancient Israel, combined in its scope rules of worship, norms of moral conduct, and the legal ordinances of the nation. All alike indiscriminately were regarded as the express commands of Jehovah. The conception of their national god as a god of righteousness gave a peculiar prominence to the ethical portion of these commands. We find, therefore, the Decalogue combining, as it does, the fundamental principles of religion and the most essential moral norms, early regarded as the core of the Hebrew code, and after the early Christians had freed them-

2

selves from the trammels of the old ceremonial law, the 'Thou shalt' and the 'Thou shalt not' of Sinai still thundered in the consciences of men as the veritable law of God.

2. A second fact which had an influence in giving a jural form to Christian conception of morality was the three centuries of hostility and practical separation between Christianity and the Empire.

In its attitude toward the state Christianity presents a marked contrast to both Judaism and paganism. The conqueror of the nations had a place for the gods of all the nations conquered. · But Christianity was not a national religion and the Roman government could find no place for it. Its aim was to establish a kingdom not of this world, a spiritual kingdom which the rulers of this world could not understand. The clear demarkation of the two fields of duty in the principle of the founder, 'render unto Cæsar the things that are Cæsar's and unto God the things that are God's,' presented a distinction between religion and jurisprudence that was wholly foreign to ancient philosophy and statecraft. This distinction in thought became an actuality in practice during the centuries of persecution to which the new religion was subject.⅂ Even when Christianity became the religion of the state, the result was rather to free the state from the cumbersome formalities of the ancient religion, than to impose upon it any new ones.[1] However later ecclesiastics might endeavor to subordinate the temporal to the spiritual, the distinction in thought at least was never lost sight of, and we have again to-day in this country, if not in Europe, the separation of Church and State in practice as well as in theory.

Now during this period of antagonism between the Christians and the Empire, they made a constant effort to have just as little as possible to do with the secular courts. The Hebrew scriptures were regarded as revealing a divine code of laws, and by means of this code the Christians constituted themselves 'an ordered community essentially distinct from

---

[1] "Christianity is the first religion that did not claim to be the source of law"—last chapter of De Coulanges, *The Ancient City*.

the state.' This very separation from the jurisprudence of the state served to stamp upon the peculiar moral maxims of Christianity a jural form, since for the first three hundred years they had actually taken the place of all civil law. The use of penances and excommunication as temporal sanctions of the divine law intensified the legal aspect of Christian ethics.

In comparison with Greek ethics, Sidgwick says that "the first point to be noticed as novel is the conception of morality as the positive law of a theocratic community, possessing a written code imposed by divine revelation, and sanctioned by express divine promises and threatenings." [1] We have already seen that among the Greeks the unwritten laws and later the law of nature, had a highly ethical import, and were often regarded as of divine origin. But the notion of command, the expression of a will, was never more than dimly conceived in the background. These laws were principles of conduct by which alone virtue or happiness could be attained, rather than the imperatives of a divine lawgiver sanctioned by rewards and punishments. In Judaism and Christianity the notion of the imperative came into the foreground.

3. Besides the Hebrew origin and the peculiar circumstances of its early history, Christianity in the West was subject to a Roman influence which made for legalism.

The peculiar jural bent of the best Roman thought and the high success of Rome's legal institutions exerted a powerful effect on Latin Christianity. The very language was saturated with legal concepts. The mere translation of the New Testament into Latin gave to Christian doctrine a decided jural tone that had been quite unsuspected in the Greek. God was no longer the Heavenly Father of the common man, or the Universal Reason of the Greek philosopher, so much as the Moral Governor of the world bound to maintain a just government.

Besides this general influence upon Christian thought from the jural cast of the Roman mind, there was an even more specific influence from Roman law itself. The Church was

1 Sidgwick, *History of Ethics*, p. 110.

in many ways the successor and heir of the Empire and it received no heritage more valuable to itself or for modern civilization than the civil code of the Eternal City. The ecclesiastical authorities not only exerted all their influence over the Teutonic invaders towards maintaining Roman jurisprudence, but they adopted the Roman law as the Canon law of the Church.

§ 8. All of these legalizing influences had had time to work their full effect on Christian thought when a century after the revival of the scientific study of Roman law at Bologna "a genuinely philosophic intellect, trained by a full study of the greatest Greek thinker, undertook to give complete scientific form to the ethical doctrines of the Catholic Church."[1] In the ethics of Thomas Aquinas, as indeed in his whole philosophy in general, there is an attempt to combine and harmonize the teachings of the New Testament and the Church Fathers with those of the Greek philosophers, or more specifically still, to harmonize Augustine as the representative of Christian doctrine with Aristotle as 'the philosopher ' *par excellence.*

In this system the notion of law occupies a highly prominent, if not the first place. It was the influence of Aristotle, doubtless, that led Aquinas to give the first place in his system to the doctrine of goods and virtues. The most complete statement of his moral philosophy is given in the first part of the second division of the *Summa Theologica.* He begins with a discussion of the chief good which he finds to be the blessedness of union with God. He next treats of the virtues and following 'the philosopher' divides them into intellectual and moral. The moral virtues again are classified into the natural or acquired and the theologic or instilled. Those virtues which may be acquired by the natural man are the four cardinal virtues of the Greeks, Prudence, Temperance, Fortitude, and Justice. Besides these, as necessary to the highest end of man, communion with God, are the three theologic virtues which are instilled in men by divine grace—Faith, Hope, and Love. This analysis of the virtues is followed by

1 Sidgwick, *History of Ethics*, p. 110.

a subtle discussion of sin and then the subject of law is taken up.[1] Thomas defines law as "an ordinance of reason for the common good which is promulgated by him who has charge of the community."[2]   Four kinds of law are distinguished—eternal, natural, human, and divine.

The *eternal law* is the divine reason of the supreme governor of the universe by which all creatures, rational and irrational are ruled.   This law, in so far as it applies to rational creatures, is given to them in two ways—naturally and by special revelation.   Hence the two kinds, natural and divine, corresponding to the two modes by which the law is made known to men.   A portion of the eternal law God has so implanted in men's minds as to be known by natural reason.[3]   This is the *law of nature*.   All rational action aims at some good.   The first principle, therefore, of natural law is that good should be done and sought, and evil avoided. Upon this principle are founded all the other precepts of the law of nature for the sake of whatever the practical reason naturally apprehends to be human goods.[4]   *Human laws* are the special rules of particular communities deduced by the reason from the precepts of natural law.   The process of the practical reason is the same as that of the speculative reason; both proceed from certain principles to certain conclusions. " Just as in the speculative reason from indemonstrable principles naturally known are drawn conclusions of different sciences, with the knowledge of which we are not naturally endowed, but which is found out by the industry of reason ; so also from the precepts of natural law, as if from certain

---

1 For a brief account of Thomas's ethics see Sidgwick, *History of Ethics*, p. 140 ff; also Ziegler, *Geschichte der Christlichen Ethik*, p. 282, ff.

2 Thomas Aquinas, *Summa Theologica*, Prima Secundae, Quaest. xc., Art. IV. " Et sic ex quatuor praedictis potest colligi definitio legis, quae nihil est aliud quam *quaedam rationis ordinatio ad bonum commune, et ab eo qui curam communitatis habet, promulgata.*"

3 " Promulgatio legis naturae est ex hoc ipso quod Deus eam mentibus hominum inseruit naturaliter cognoscendam."   Qu. xc., Art. IV.   " Lex naturalis nihil aliud est quam participatio legis aeternae in rationali creatura."   Qu. xci., Art. II.

4 Ibid. Qu. xciv., Art. II.

common and indemonstrable principles, it is necessary that the human reason proceed to more particular rules, and these are human laws provide the other conditions determinative of law be observed." [1]

Unjust laws, i. e., such as are contrary to human good, are not binding in the forum of conscience, though for the sake of avoiding scandal and disturbance, it may be better to obey them. But laws contrary to divine good are in no wise to be observed.[2] We ought to obey God rather than man. All inferior governors derive their authority from the eternal law of the supreme governor. Human law, therefore, in so far as it accords with right reason, is derived from eternal law.[3]

Obedience to the law of nature suffices for attaining to the natural or acquired virtues. Since, however, man is ordained to an end higher than the natural, it is necessary for the direction of human life that we have besides natural and human law *divine law* given by God to men by special revelation. This divine law is double[4]—the one revealed in the Old Testament through the instrumentality of angels, the other in the New Testament by God himself made man. The old law seeks sensible and terrestrial good, the new one intelligible and celestial good. The first summoned the people to the earthly kingdom of the Canaanites, the latter to the kingdom of heaven. The old promises temporal things, the new promises eternal life. The old controls the hand, the new the mind. The motive of the old was fear, of the new love. Of the old law the ceremonial and judicial precepts are no longer obligatory, but the moral precepts, particularly as given in the Decalogue, are still binding upon Christians. The new law is variously designated as the law of the Gospel, law of love, law of grace, etc. Besides giving commands it also confers upon the faithful strength for the fulfilment of these commands. The divine

1 Ibid. Qu. xci., Art. III.
2 Ibid. Qu. xcvi., Art. IV.
3 Ibid. Qu. xciii., Art. III.
4 These two laws are not related to each other as two species, e. g., horse and cow, but as the imperfect to the perfect, e. g., boy and man. Qu. xci , Art. V.

law is ordained to secure the communion of men with God. To its positive commands "without which the order of virtue, which is the order of reason, could not be observed," it adds as counsels the monastic virtues of poverty, celibacy, and obedience, which, though not obligatory, afford a superior means for attaining to the perfect life.[1]

In Thomas Aquinas we have the culmination and epitome of Scolasticism, "the crowning result of the great constructive effort of mediæval philosophy."[2] His influence has been very great, both on the theology of the Catholics, by whom he is still regarded as the official philosopher of the Church, and also on the theology of Protestants. The part which the jural view of morality plays in his ethical system illustrates very fairly the position of this view in Christian ethics in general. The Decalogue, with its never-failing appeal to the moral consciousness, has been to Christians and to all who have come under the influence of Christianity the preëminent summary of moral principles, and, being expressed as the command of God, it has appeared as a moral law. Thus the notion of morality as a code of laws has been deeply stamped on popular thought and in only a slightly less degree on the would be scientific systems of ethical philosophers. Morality and obedience to the Ten Commandments are to many almost synonymous terms, and this fact, together with the other influences already mentioned, has given a prominently jural form to the ethics of the Church in all ages—in modern times as well as in the Middle Ages.

1 " Lex divina convenienter proponit praecepta de actibus omnium virtutum, . . . but yet quaedam sine quibus ordo virtutis, qui est ordo rationis, observari non potest, cadunt sub obligatione praecepti; quaedam vero quae pertinent ad bene esse virtutis perfectas, cadunt sub admonitione consilii." Qu. c., Art. II.

2 Sidgwick, *History of Ethics*, p. 147.

CHAPTER III.

§ 9. Having thus briefly sketched the influence of jural concepts in ancient and mediæval ethics, we come now to modern systems. Mediæval philosophy was characterized by submission to authority—on the one hand to the Church, and on the other to Aristotle. Modern philosophy yields to no authority, but facing freely the problems of the universe, seeks a solution which shall force irresistible conviction upon every intelligence. In the modern attempt to establish morality on an independent foundation, *i. e.*, independent of special revelation and of ecclesiastical authority, the notion of the law of nature was the first principle seized upon. If we examine the moral philosophy of Aquinas two points present themselves on which conceivably an independent, rational morality might be founded—(1) the acquired virtues, (2) the law of nature. It was the latter of these principles which actually served as the starting point of modern ethics.

After the combined influences of Renaissance and Reformation had effectually undermined the traditional confidence in the old authorities, the need of a new ethics was first felt in politics. Wherever there was a difference of faith between king and subjects, a new question as to the duties of allegiance was raised, and now that the general supremacy of the Pope over the nations was no longer recognized a new theory was required to determine the relations and duties of independent states to one another. It was for the purpose of solving the problems arising from the changed relations of nations that Grotius composed his epoch-making work, *De Jure Belli et Pacis*[1]—the work which is universally recog-

1 Paris, 1625.

nized as the foundation of the modern system of International Law. The basis on which he erected his system was the old Stoic theory of the law of nature as it had been handed down by the Roman jurists and ecclesiastical moralists.

Grotius defines natural law as the " dictate of Right Reason, indicating that an act, from its agreement or disagreement with man's rational and social nature, is morally disgraceful or morally necessary." [1] Here we find the law of nature defined in a manner broad enough to include a moral as well as a legal code. According to the theory of Grotius, though God is the creator of nature and her laws, yet the nature of things when once created remains ever after unchangeable and unaffected by the divine will. In the nature of man, then, by the use of the reason, we may find the fundamental principles of morals and jurisprudence. Now man is distinguished from other animals by his peculiar capacity for society, hence from the nature of man as a social being may be deduced the principles which should govern his conduct in society. The utility of social laws is also recognized as a secondary principle. But the utility is only secondary. Even if there were no advantage to be attained from it, man's very nature as social would require him to submit to the laws of society. Since now these are laws of man's nature itself, they are binding upon him in the natural state before he has united with his fellows and by an "express or tacit pact" formed a state. Just as individuals, while in the state of nature and as yet subject to no sovereign power, were nevertheless bound by the laws of nature, so modern nations which are related to each other like persons independent of any authority, are still under obligation to observe the laws of nature in their dealings with one another.[2]

1 Sidgwick, *History of Ethics*, p. 160.

2 " The grandest function of the Law of Nature was discharged in giving birth to modern International Law and to the modern Law of War." Maine, *Ancient Law*, p. 96.

For a brief account of Grotius and his place in the history of ethics see Jodl, *Geschichte der Ethik in der neueren Philosophie*, Bd. I., Cap. III., Absch. 5.

§ 10. ⸀The theory of the state propounded by Thomas Hobbes may be regarded as the beginning of independent ethics in England. Beyond a few pregnant suggestions Bacon had done little in moral philosophy. The current view of the law of nature furnished Hobbes with a starting point. But while employing much the same language his theory of morals is in essence almost the antithesis of that of Grotius. In both men the aim was to establish a theory of the state, and they concern themselves with ethics only so far as is necessary for this purpose. While the chief aim of Grotius's work was to determine the relations of independent states, Hobbes devoted himself to determining the relations of sovereign and subject in the same state. Both seek a foundation for their theories in morals, but while Grotius· finds that in the social impulses of man's nature, itself, Hobbes regards man by nature as impelled only by self-interest and all moral norms as springing from the state and the civil law. The ethical speculations involved in Hobbes's theory of the state and the attacks called out in opposition determined the development of moral philosophy in England for nearly a century. –

Ths psychological basis of Hobbes's theory is frankly egotistic. "Of the voluntary acts of every man the object is some Good to himself." [1] Since man naturally seeks only his own satisfaction the original state of nature was a condition of war of every man against every other man. In this state of affairs there was no law and no morality. "The desires and other passions of man are in themselves no sin. No more are the actions that proceed from those passions, till they know a law that forbids them; which till laws be made they cannot know, nor can any law be made till they have agreed upon the person that shall make it. . . . To this war of every man against every man, this also is consequent; that nothing can be unjust. The notions of right and wrong, justice and injustice, have there no place. Where there is no common power, there is no law; where no law,

---

[1] Hobbes, *Leviathan*, p. 66. (I quote from Thornton's reprint, giving the pages of the original edition of 1651.)

no injustice. Force and Fraud are in war the two cardinal virtues. Justice and injustice are none of the faculties, neither of the body nor mind." [1] Reason, however, is no less of the nature of man than passion, and since this is the same in all men, directing them to seek their own good, there can be no other law of nature than reason. Accordingly Hobbes defines the law of nature as a "precept, or general rule, found out by reason, by which a man is forbidden to do that which is destructive of his life, or taketh away the means of preserving the same ; and to omit that by which he thinketh it may be best preserved." [2] From this definition is deduced the fundamental law of nature '*to seek peace and follow it*,' and failing in this '*by all means we can to defend ourselves.*' Such rights as being retained hinder the peace of mankind ought to be given up, if we can be assured that others will do the same. This gives us a second law of nature, and from it follows the third, which is 'that men perform their covenants made.' [3] The validity of the covenant depends upon the assurance that it will be observed. 'Therefore before the names just and unjust can have place, there must be some coercive power to compel men equally to the performance of their covenants, by the terror of some punishment greater than the benefit they expect by the breach of their covenant ; . . . and such power there is none before the erection of a commonwealth.' Justice is the 'keeping of covenant,' and, as this is a rule of reason by which we are forbidden to do anything destructive to our life, it is consequently a law of nature.

From these primary laws of nature Hobbes goes on to deduce a number of others ; in fact he makes nineteen in all, but to 'leave all men unexcusable, they have been contracted into one easy sum, intelligible even to the meanest capacity ; and that is, Do not that to another which thou wouldest not have done to thyself.' [4] These laws are always binding

1 Ibid. pp. 62, 63.
2 Ibid. p. 64.
3 Ibid. p. 71.
4 Ibid. p. 79.

on our desires and intentions, but we are under no obligation
to put them in act unless we have a reasonable assurance
that others will observe the same laws towards us. 'The
laws of nature are immutable and eternal,' for these are the
precepts of peace and 'it can never be that war shall pre-
serve life and peace destroy it.'[1] All of these precepts may
be termed indifferently laws of nature, as being the dictates
of natural reason, or moral laws 'because they concern men's
manners and conversations one toward another,' or, again, divine laws 'in respect of the author thereof, God Almighty.'[2]
The true doctrine of the laws of nature Hobbes declares to
be 'the true and only moral philosophy.'

In order that men may enjoy the blessings of peace as natural reason dictates, there must be a sovereign power capable
of enforcing obedience to compacts. The only way to erect
such a power is by mutual consent to confer the power and
strength of all upon one man or upon one assembly of men
that may reduce all their wills unto one will. In this way a
real unity of them all is established in one and the same person.[3] 'The right of all sovereigns is derived originally from
the consent of every one of those that are to be governed ;
whether they that choose him do it for their common defence
against an enemy, as when they agree among themselves to
appoint a man or assembly of men to protect them ; or
whether they do it to save their lives by submission to a con-
quering enemy.'[4] After the sovereign power is once established it is the duty of every one to yield implicit obedience
to it in all matters. The sovereign is under obligation only
to God and the laws of nature. The civil laws which he in-
stitutes are to determine without question the conduct of the
subject. They are to him the ultimate standard of right and
wrong, good and evil. 'By the law of nature the civil sov-

---

1 Besides these laws of nature which dictate peace and are necessary to
the existence of civil society, whatever tends 'to the destruction of particular men as drunkenness and all other parts of intemperance,' Hobbes
regards as forbidden by the law of nature.

2 Hobbes, *Elements of Law*, Pt. I, Chap. 18.

3 *Leviathan*, p. 87.

4 Ibid. p. 314.

ereign in every commonwealth is the head, the source, the root, and the sun from which all jurisdiction is derived'[1]— ecclesiastical as well as political. It is heresy for a private person to maintain any doctrine prohibited by the state.[2] Thus while the laws of nature served Hobbes as the theoretical basis of the state, the criterion of morality for the individual, according to his doctrine, is the positive civil law. To obey the laws of the state is the whole duty of man, ethical and religious.

In a double way, therefore, the ethics of Hobbes takes on a jural aspect in its fundamental theory, being based on the *laws* of nature, and in its practical outcome referring all determinations of duty to the civil law. The jural elements in this theory are widely different from the divine commands of Paley's system or the categorical imperative of Kant's. In fact the laws of nature are for Hobbes's jural only in the mode of expression and not at all in the concept itself. The phrase 'law of nature' was one held in high respect by jurists, ecclesiastics, and rationalists. It was, therefore, a very advantageous phrase for the founder of a new theory of the state to have continually in his mouth. Hobbes himself is careful to state that he does not in reality attach any jural significance to the term. At the end of the two chapters[3] of the *Leviathan,* which he devotes particularly to the definition and deduction of the natural laws, he says:

" These dictates of reason men use to call by the name of laws, but improperly, for they are but conclusions, or theorems concerning what conduceth to the conversation and defense of themselves; whereas law properly is the word of him that by right hath command over others. But yet if we consider the same theorems as delivered in the Word of God, that by right commandeth all things, then are they properly called laws."[4] The reference of the laws to God serves simply to explain the term, and perhaps is intended also to

1 Ibid. p. 312.
2 Ibid. p. 317.
3 XIV. and XV.
4 Ibid. p. 80.

conciliate religious sentiments, but it is quite outside the line of argument of the theory itself.

§ 11.   Such a system as that of Hobbes's 'in which the only fixed positions were selfishness everywhere and unlimited power somewhere' could but excite the strongest opposition from the moral sense and liberty loving spirit of the English people.   While the absoluteness of the sovereign power offended the liberals in politics, the making of selfregarding motives the only determinants of conduct and the civil law the standard of good and evil aroused the antagonism of moral philosophers.   Each of these three points, the absolutism of the state, the egoism and relativism of morality called out answers from moralists.   Locke championed the natural rights of the individual citizen, Cumberland maintained that the common good of all is the supreme end and standard of conduct, and Cudworth taught that moral principals are eternal and immutable.

In the writings of Cudworth, who was the foremost of the Cambridge Platonists, we find a noteworthy opposition to jural conceptions of morality.   In his view neither civil law nor divine law can determine morality.   Good and evil are essentially and eternally distinct, and no mere will, not even that of God Himself, can alter this distinction.   Surely the transitory and changeable laws of the state cannot be the source of that which in its nature is eternal and unchangeable.   Moral truths are immutable ideas of the divine reason and, like the truths of mathematics, are apprehended by the human reason, and are, therefore, equally valid for all rational beings.   In the ethics of Locke and Cumberland, however, we find the jural concepts again regnant.   Both of these philosophers treated morality as a code of laws promulgated by God, revealed in the natural reason and sanctioned by rewards and punishments.   "Moral good and evil," says Locke, "is only the conformity or disagreement of our voluntary actions to some law, whereby good and evil is drawn on us by the will and power of the law-maker; which good and evil, pleasure or pain, attending our observance or breach of the law, by the decree of the law-maker, is that

we call reward and punishment."[1]   These sanctions are insisted upon by Locke as absolutely essential to morality.   It
is only ' by rewards and punishments that will overbalance the
satisfaction any one shall propose to himself in the breach
of the law,' that moral laws have the power to curb and re-
strain inordinate desires.[2]   Locke distinguished three classes
of laws : (1) divine laws, (2) civil laws, (3) laws of opinion or
reputation.[3] Virtue and vice in general are the names given
to such actions as receive the approval or disapproval of
public opinion, but when these names ' stand for actions in
their own nature right and wrong,' then they are ' coincident
with the divine, law.'[3]   The moral laws are not innate in
the human mind, but they are ' knowable by the light of
nature,' and it is, therefore, ' our own fault if we come not
to a certain knowledge of them.'[4]   For Locke, as for all the
philosophers of the 17th century, mathematics was the
ideal science, and mathematical demonstration the type of
certainty.   Moral truths he believed to be equally necessary
and capable of demonstration, though on account of their
complexity and the impossibility of presenting them to the
eye by diagrams, their demonstration is more difficult.[5]

Cumberland[6] like Locke regarded morality as a code of
laws and as capable of demonstration as mathematics.   The
only respect in which he is of distinctive interest in this
connection is his presentation of the general welfare as the
fundamental law of nature and its essential agreement with
individual interest, in this attacking the universal selfishness
of Hobbes's system.   A law of nature in his view is " a
proposition proposed to the observation of or impressed upon
the mind with sufficient clearness by the nature of things,
from the will of the first cause, which points out that possible action of a rational agent which will chiefly promote

1 Locke, *Essay concerning Human Understanding*, Bk. II., Ch. 28, § 5.
2 Ibid. Bk. I., Ch. 3, § 13.
3 Ibid. Bk. II., Ch. 28, § 10.
4 Ibid. Bk. I., Ch. 3, § 1.
5 Ibid. Bk. IV., Ch. 3, § 18, 19.
6 His chief work, *De Legibus Naturae* (1672) shows him to have been
greatly influenced by Grotius.

the common good, and by which only the entire happiness
of particular persons can be obtained." " The greatest be-
nevolence of every rational agent towards all forms the hap-
piest state of every and of all the benevolent, as far as in
their power; and it is necessarily requisite to the happiness
which they can attain, and therefore the common good is
the supreme law."[1] As Hobbes is the founder of egoistic
hedonism in English ethics, so Cumberland is the founder
of universalistic hedonism.

The law of God which formed the ultimate authority in
morals for Locke and Cumberland was considered as knowable by natural reason and is thus to be distinguished from
the divine law of the Hebrews and mediæval moralists.
This distinction might be expressed by calling the ethics of
former *theologic* juralism, the latter *Hebraic* juralism.

§ 12. The most thorough going presentation of theologic
juralism in moral philosophy, the culmination of the ethical
theories of 'natural theology' as taught in the 17th and
18th centuries is found in the system of Paley. With him
the law of God is no mere incidental factor or theoretic
basis, but the moving principle of the whole system. The
moral law is conceived in complete analogy with civil law.
It is the express command of a lawgiver who has the
authority and power to enforce his will by rewards and punishments.   To be obliged is to be ' urged by a violent motive
resulting from the command of another,' and just as we should
not be obliged to obey the civil law except for the rewards
and punishments, the pleasures and pains dependent upon our
obedience, 'so neither should we without the same reason, be
obliged to do what is right, to practice virtue, or to obey the
commands of God.'[2] Between prudence and duty ' the difference and the only difference' is that 'in the one case we
consider what we shall gain or lose in the present world, in
the other case we consider also what we shall gain or lose
in the world to come.'[3]

  [1] Quoted from Porter's appendix to the translation of Uberweg's History
of Philosophy, Vol. II., p. 362.
  [2] Paley, *Principles of Moral and Political Philosophy*, Bk. II., Ch. 2.
  [3] Ibid. Bk. II., Ch. 3.

Not only are the moral motives, according to Paley, of a purely utilitarian nature, but the moral law itself is to be discovered by the same principle. To learn this law we need only inquire what is the will of God, for moral obligation depends upon God's will and right signifies consistency with this same will.[1] Since now the predominant tendency of the contrivance indicates the disposition of the designer, we may conclude that God wills and wishes the happiness of his creatures. In order, therefore, by the light of nature to come at the will of God concerning any action, it is only necessary for us to inquire into the tendency of this action 'to promote or diminish the general happiness.'[2] Paley's whole theory, both in its jural and in its utilitarian aspects, is summed up concisely and completely in his definition of virtue : " The doing good to mankind, in obedience to the will of God, and for the sake of everlasting happiness."[3]

In the ethical systems thus far considered we have found the law of nature, the law of God in two forms, and the law of the state playing a more or less prominent part. Natural juralism, Hebraic juralism, theologic juralism and civil juralism have one element in common ; they all involve the notion of a lawgiver apart from man who imposes laws upon him. These systems, therefore, may all be designated as *heteronomous*. We have now to consider a system which in this respect stands out in signal contrast to all of the foregoing, a system which finds the moral law in the man himself and which in distinction from the rest we may call *autonomus*. The claim of Kant to be the Copernicus of speculative philosophy may be also admitted in the field of practical philosophy. Just as he found that space and time and the laws of the physical world are not given to us from without but are imposed by us upon the world of phenomena, so he showed that the moral laws are not given to us by God or the state, but every man by virtue of his own rational nature imposes these laws upon himself.

1 Ibid. Bk. II., Ch. 9.
2 Ibid. Bk. II., Ch. 4, 5.
3 Ibid. Bk. I., Ch. 7.

3

§ 13. In the same year (1785) in which Paley's Moral
Philosophy appeared, Kant published the first of his great
ethical works, *Grundlegung zur Metaphysik der Sitten.* The
contrast between these two works is one of the most strik-
ing presented in the whole history of speculative philosophy.
Compare with Paley's definition of virtue, "the doing good
to mankind in obedience to the will of God and for the sake
of everlasting happiness," the statement of Kant that in order for an action to be morally good "it is not enough that
it conform to the moral law but it must be done for the sake
of the law."[1]

With Paley the source of the law is God, the end is human
good, the motive everlasting happiness ; with Kant the source
of the law is the pure reason, the end is not to be taken into
account at all, and the only moral motive is reverence for the
law itself.

Had nature intended man for happiness only, instinct would
have been all sufficient, but reason has a higher purpose. Its
office is to produce a will that shall be good not only as a
means to something else, but good in 'itself. In fact nothing
in the world can be conceived as unconditionally good but
the Good Will.[2] All other goods are but means only. The
good will is an end in itself and to the production of such a
will reason is absolutely necessary. The moral law must
have its seat in the pure reason. None of the peculiar circumstances of man's nature are to be taken into account lest
some empirical taint sully the *a priori* purity of the law. That
law only is truly moral which is valid for every rational being as such. Hence it is the pure reason alone apart from
all the interests of particular beings that can be the lawgiver.
Thus the law is imposed by each man upon himself and is at
the same time valid for all rational beings. Only such a law
can command the respect of men, and however they may fail
to obey it, they nevertheless instinctively reverence it. Were
the law conditioned by inclination or imposed by any power

1 From the preface to the *Grundlegung zur Metaphysik der Sitten,*
Abbott's translation of Kant's ethical works, p. 4.
2 Ibid. p. 9.

outside of ourselves, obedience to it would produce only legality and not morality. To be of moral worth an act must be done *from duty*. Even though the effects of the action be quite in accord with duty, it cannot be regarded as moral unless it is done solely from duty or respect for the law. The act done from duty possesses the same moral worth whether its effects be useful or injurious. Particularly must the act have no regard to inclinations. Indeed it is only in cases where we act directly contrary to inclinations that we can be perfectly sure that we are acting morally at all. If inclination and duty command the same act there will be a doubt whether we do the act solely from duty, and it is only in so far as done from duty alone that the act is worthy to be designated as moral.

Our knowledge of the moral law, the principles of the practical reason is obtained just like the knowledge of all rational principles. "We become conscious of pure practical laws just as we are conscious of pure theoretical principles, by attending to the necessity with which reason prescribes them, and to the elimination of all empirical conditions." [1] "The moral law is given as a fact of pure reason of which we are *a priori* conscious, and which is apodictically certain, though it be granted that in experience no example of its exact fulfilment can be found." [2] "All moral conceptions have their seat and origin completely *a priori* in the reason and that, moreover, in the commonest reason just as truly as in that which is in the highest degree speculative." [3]

The formula for the rational principle which is to determine the will of an imperfect being is called an imperative. If the imperative commands an action good only as a means to something else, it is called a hypothetical imperative. If, however, the action is conceived as good in itself and consequently as being necessarily the principle of a will which of itself conforms to reason, then it is categorical. Hypo-

1 *Kritik der praktischen Vernunft*, Bk. I., Ch. I, § VI., Abbott's translation, p. 118.

2 Ibid. p. 136.

3 *Grundlegung zur Metaphysik der Sitten*, trans. p. 28.

thetical imperatives are rules of skill or counsels of prudence; only a categorical imperative can be a law of morality. Duty as a practical, unconditional necessity of action must hold good for all rational beings and so for all human wills. The fundamental formula of the moral law, the categorical imperative is : "Act so that the maxim of thy will can always at the same time hold good as a principle of universal legislation . " [1] or, in other words, make a law which you could will to be universal the rule of your conduct. Since man and generally any rational being exists as an end in himself, not merely as a means to be arbitrarily used by this or that will, a secondary form of the categorical imperative is : "So act as to treat humanity, whether in thine own person or in that of another, in every case as an end withal, never as means only." [2] In renouncing all individual interests the will becomes universally legislative and thus acquires for humanity the highest possible dignity. The moral will is subject only to the laws of which it can regard itself as author. " Looking back now," says Kant, "upon all previous attempts to discover the principles of morality, we need not wonder why they all failed. It was seen that man was bound to law by duty, but it was not observed that the laws to which he is subject are only those of his own giving, though at the same time they are universal, and that he is only bound to act in conformity with his own will; a will, however, which is designed by nature to give universal laws." [3]

In the present century the tendency of ethics on the whole has been away from the jural type. The phrase 'Moral Law' however, has continued to occupy a prominent place in ethical discussions. The popular conception of morality as the command of the deity, the long and honorable history of the term in philosophy, the majesty of the civil law, the appropriateness of the term to express the unconditioned necessity of moral duties—all of these circumstances combine to keep the term in use even though it is regarded

1 *Kritik der praktischen Vernunft*, Bk. I., Ch. I., § VII., trans. p. 119.
2 *Grundlegung zur Metaphysik der Sitten*, trans. p. 47.
3 Ibid. p. 51.

as only a metaphor. Perhaps, too, the respect for the word law, arising from its use in the physical sciences, has made moralists who retain little of the old jural sense of the term still cling to the word. "Metaphors from law and metaphors from war," says Bagehot, "make most of our current moral phrases, and a nice examination would easily explain that both rather vitiate what both often illustrate."[1] The 'metaphors from law,' however, will doubtless long continue to furnish the most effective means for popular instruction in morals, and if the different senses of the term be carefully distinguished perhaps no more useful term can be found for the ethical scientist.

[1] Bagehot, *Physics and Politics*, p. 79.

CHAPTER IV.

THE MORAL LAW.

§ 14. In all the sciences of to-day the term law plays an important part. While the one term is used with equal freedom in all, the corresponding concept takes on almost as many different forms as there are different sciences. We hear continually such expressions as laws of chemistry, laws of motion, laws of logic, laws of poetry, laws of the state, laws of etiquette, etc. Among all these various uses of the term we may distinguish two typical forms of the concept : (1) law in jurisprudence, (2) law in physics. The first is the original form of the concept, the second a derived form. All the other uses of the term are varieties of one or the other of these fundamental species of the concept, or else more or less confused combinations of the two.

"The term law," says Zeller, "in all languages meant originally a rule of conduct established by some person, whether human or divine, with regard to the conduct of men ; a law is what the community requires or the deity commands."[1] It is precisely in this same sense that we use the term to-day in jurisprudence. Holland gives the definition : "A law is a general rule of external human action enforced by a sovereign political authority."[2] This form of the concept involves three essential elements. To see these clearly we may state the definition thus : a law is (1) a rule of conduct which (2) a will in authority imposes upon (3) a subject will.

1 Zeller, *Vorträge und Abhandlungen, 3 Samm. p. 189.*
2 Holland, *Elements of Jurisprudence*, p. 37.

(1) The essence of this first element, rule of conduct, is *uniformity in action.* Without prescribed rules one man may act in one way, another in another, or the same man in different ways at different times. Wherever uniformity is observed in the conduct of men, it is abscribed to laws of some kind, as the laws of the state, laws of custom, laws of nature, etc. Thus the law is an expression of uniformity in action. (2) This rule of action is always thought of as established by some power in authority. Hence as a second element we must recognize the *legislative will.* (3) The rule of action is laid upon some person *i. e.*, upon a free will, who may or may not conform to it. The freedom of the subject, or the *possibility of non-conformity* is always contemplated in this sense of the term. This first typical form of the concept involves, therefore, these three essential elements : uniformity in action, a legislative will, and freedom or the possibility of non-conformity on the part of the subject.

As the Greeks became better acquainted with other nations, especially after the conquests of Alexander, they found many of the same rules of conduct in force among the barbarians as among themselves. These common norms and customs, they saw, could not have been established by the lawgiver of any one city or people. Common to all men, they must have been established by a power having authority over all men in common. The legislative will became now Zeus, Nature or the divine creative Reason. In Sophocles, as we have seen, the unwritten laws of the gods are clearly distinguished from the written laws of human kings. Heracleitus connected this divine law with the order of things in nature. The Stoics were the first, however, to bring into general use the term law as applied to the natural order of things. They believed that the ultimate cause of the world was not merely a material substance, but also a creative power and Reason. The natural order and necessity in the universe they explained as the expression of the will of that Ultimate Reason. They used the phrase law of nature indifferently for the order in the physical world and for the principles of moral conduct. In the Stoic concept of law of nature as applied to the external world we find the element of uniformity of action as in the first form, the legislative will broadened into a universal Reason, but the third element that of freedom, completely vanishes. In this case the law is not imposed upon persons who may or may not obey, but upon inert matter which always conforms to the law necessarily.

The elimination of the second element converts the Stoic concept into the modern scientific idea of natural law. The legislative will as well as the possibility of non-conformity has disappeared and we have left only the first element—uniformity in action. The metaphysical philosopher may still resort to an ultimate rational will to explain the order in nature, but the physicist as such uses the term law without any implications of a lawgiver. To him the law is the expression for the mode of action in things, not for something outside of things. It is simply the statement of the fact of a certain uniformity in nature. The general form of a law in physics is: under certain conditions, certain events always happen. This unexceptional validity of the physical law is its characteristic mark. Of the three essential elements in the jural sense of the term we find only one in the physical law, viz., uniformity in action.

What now is the relation of the concept moral law to these two typical forms of law?

The moral laws are those rules of conduct which we feel ourselves under obligation to obey. Briefly put, the moral law is the code of duties. In this general formal definition all moralists would agree, I think. It is in regard to the source, end, scope, and content of the code of duties that the schools differ. According to the Hebraic or the theological conception of morality these norms of conduct are laid upon man by the divine lawgiver. In this case the moral law is of precisely the same type as civil law. The three elements of this type are all present—the prescribed uniformity of conduct, the legislative will, and the subject will. Or, if with Hobbes we regard the state, or, with certain recent writers, society or humanity as the source of the law, we find the same essential agreement with the jural form of the concept.

But, as Kant has so well shown, any command which is put upon us by an external will can have of itself only the force of *legality*. It acquires the force of *morality*, obedience to it became a duty and not merely a matter of prudence, only as we bind it upon ourselves and it is brought by self under the feeling of obligation. [No imperatives of parents, the state, or even of divine revelation, could command anything but a prudential, legal conformity, unless at the same time they appealed to the inner sense of duty. Such externally imposed imperatives may well be the *ratio cognoscendi;* but never of themselves the *ratio essendi* of the moral law. "It is the very essence of moral duty to be imposed by a man upon himself. . . . What we primarily understand by 'law' is some sort of command given by a superior in power to one whom he is able to punish for disobedience; whereas it is the essence of moral 'law' that it is a rule which a man imposes on himself, and from another motive than the fear of punishment. . . . The spirit of man sets before him the ideal of a perfect life, and pronounces obedience to the positive law to be necessary to its realization."[1] Thus in morality the legislative will is one with the subject will. But the concept of law still remains of the same general type. We still have the three elements of law as in jurisprudence.

While the term law in ethics is generally used as above described in the jural sense, we should not forget the existence of laws in the physical sense. In moral phenomena we find certain uniformities of sequence as well as in physical phenomena. Conduct and character are causally related, and their relation it would seem possible to express by general formulas, i. e., by laws. The general form of such a natural law of ethics is : such and such conduct produces such and such states of consciousness and such and such character. Selfishness brings unhappiness—violation of duty is followed by stings of conscience—lying degrades character;

1 T. H. Green, *Prolegomena to Ethics*, p. 354.

these are examples of laws in the moral sphere in just the same sense and of just the same validity and necessity as the facts that ice melts at 32 degrees and that a falling body increases in velocity as the square of the distance. Spencer says: "I conceive it to be the business of Moral Science to deduce from the laws of life and the conditions of existence what kinds of action necessarily tend to produce happiness, and what kinds to produce unhappiness. Having done this, its deductions are to be recognized as laws of conduct."[1] Now without making this the whole business of ethics, it is certainly a part of its work to discover the 'laws of conduct.' We may not believe as Mr. Spencer seems to, that these laws can be deduced from biology. We may have to discover them empirically rather than deductively. We may, too, be more interested to know what sort of conduct makes for perfection of character or for the 'health of the social tissue,' but at any rate besides investigating ends and motives ethics must formulate the laws of conduct by which these ends if chosen may be attained. In logic and æsthetics, and indeed in all the practical sciences, we find this same double use of the term law. The laws of logic as statements of the mind's procedure in thinking are necessary sequences of the same type as physical laws. But when from these laws of thought we form rules of argument we have imperatives which we bind upon ourselves in view of certain ends, i. e., laws in the jural sense of the concept. So, too, in æsthetics from the principles of beauty we derive rules of art, and use the term law indiscriminately for both the principles and the rules. Since these two widely different concepts are both expressed by the one term law, and since we have laws of both types in morals, ethical writers have often confused them. Where the context does not make the meaning of the word perfectly clear, ambiguity might be avoided by the use of *imperatives* for one sense and *uniformities* for the other.

§ 15. On the basis of this analysis of the concept of law

1 Spencer, *Data of Ethics*, p. 57.

in ethics, we will make a brief examination of the source, ends, and motives of the moral law.

In one sense of the term the moral laws as psychical uniformities are constitutive principles of man's being, a part of his very nature. To ask for their source could have no other meaning than to ask the source of the man himself. The origin of the moral principles of man's nature demands no special explanation apart from that of the intellectual or any other class of powers of the human spirit. To explain the origin of the moral consciousness would seem to involve essentially the same difficulties to the evolutionist, neither less nor more, than to explain the origin of the intellectual consciousness, and should an evolutionary origin be accepted it can no more invalidate the duties of the former than the truths of the latter.

The fundamental source of the moral *imperatives* is these constitutive principles of man's moral nature. They are not given to him from without but are the expression of the character of his inmost being. Not in these principles taken absolutely, however, is the source of imperatives to be sought, but in them as related to the whole man, and the man too as related to society and the universe in general. Man is to live and develop the capacities of the nature which he has and in the relations in which he finds himself. Morality is a certain function of the relation which the individual self sustains to the world. This might be expressed in a *quasi* mathematical formula as follows :

$$M = f\left(\frac{S}{W}\right)$$

This is indeed a highly complicated ratio, for the S, the individual, is both physical and spiritual in his nature, and in the W is included not only the physical world but the animal kingdom, society and the invisible, eternal, spiritual reality of things. The due adjustment of this complex ratio, as far as it lies within our power, is the problem of moral conduct. The moral law is the code of rules derived from the study of this relationship and imposed upon the individual by his own sense of duty.

By far the largest and most important part of this problem, the part most fully in our own power, consists in the
adjustment of the individual to society. The historical development of this adjustment has furnished us with the
greater part of our present moral code. Lawgivers and
moral reformers have doubtless had a large influence upon
the evolution of moral norms. But the continual interaction
of man upon man and the attitude of rulers and the state
toward the individual, in short society has been the control-
ing element in establishing the moral laws that are generally
recognized. Our actual code of morals has not been given
by revelation, discovered by intuition, or deduced by a conscious study of man's relation to the world, but it is the
product of the historical interaction of individuals and society upon one another.   Had man not come into social relations the sense of duty would probably have lain dormant
in the human breast.   It is society that has actualized and
brought to light the latent morality of mankind.   In man's
moral nature as developed by society, therefore, we find the
source of the moral law. Nor is the law any the less binding
because it is the product of evolution.   As has often been
remarked, to explain the origin of a thing is not to explain it
away.   The keenest analysis leaves the sense of duty, the
feeling of obligation, as an ultimate, irreducable fact.   Such
being the case we must admit that the moral imperatives
are at bottom not hypothetical but categorical *in form.* But
while we find Kant and the intuitionists right as to the form
of the law, the empiricists are equally right as to the content.   Men of moral sanity feel within themselves the categorical imperative to do duty, or, stated one degree less ab-
stractly, to will the good.   But as to what is duty, or what is
the good to be willed, only experience can tell us.

§ 16.   Accepting the command —Will the good — as the
simplest and most comprehensive statement of the moral
law, we must at once raise the questions, Whose good and
which good ?   The end of the moral law must accordingly
be examined from these two standpoints: What are the

goods aimed at and who are to receive these goods? We will consider the latter question first.

Good is a relative term and has no meaning apart from some sentient being who is to experience it. Who, then, is the sentient being whose good is aimed at by the moral law? Or, to use a German phrase, who is the end-subject (*zweck-subject*) of morality? There are three possible answers to this question, animals, men, God. We cannot admit the last as a proper end-subject of our morality. Accepting the fullest theistic conception of God, we cannot suppose him to be wanting in anything which our acts can supply. Regarding him as the lawgiver and as most sympathetically interested in us as his children, still he is not the end-subject of our conduct. In saying this we would not be understood as in any degree belittling the importance of religious duties. These duties are a part of the objective end of the moral law, but they are due to society and to ourselves as spiritual beings, rather than to God as their end-subject. We take the medicine that the physician prescribes not for his sake, but for the sake of our own health.

Are animals end-subjects of our moral acts? Yes, in so far as they are susceptible to weal at our hands. Modern abhorrence of cruelty to animals may be explained by the belief that one who is cruel to dogs and horses will also be cruel to men in his power. Were it not, however, that the horse is sentient and therefore so far deserving of our sympathy, beating his horse would not beget cruelty in his driver. We may justly fear that the boy who has no regard for the pains of the pony he rides will grow up devoid of sympathy for the sufferings of his fellow men. However hard the boy may lash his whip about a post, we do not think that he is thereby acquiring the habit of cruelty. The pony is sentient and the post is not. The boy who beats his pony is acquiring the habit of cruelty because he is violating the duty to further the good of sentient beings. The degree to which any being is susceptible to weal at our hands determines the extent of our duty to it. The father of a family has not the same duty to the babe in arms as to the son of

ten or to the daughter of twenty.   In the case of the lower
animals our duty is of course very small.   A proper satisfaction of their physical needs, infliction of no unnecessary pain,
and in the case of certain of the finest breeds of domestic
animals a gentleness and kindliness of tone in their presence, make up perhaps the sum total of our duties to animals.   A recognition of duties to animals in so far as they
are susceptible to weal does not, as Ihering, for example,
maintains, preclude the slaughter of animals for food or vivi-
section in the cause of science.   We do not hesitate to justify
the infliction of pain on our own bodies for a greater good.
If life or health demand it, we suffer any surgical operation,
however painful, and for the greater good to man we are
justified in inflicting pain upon and taking the lives of lower
animals.

While we thus regard animals as true end-subjects of our
duties as far as they are susceptible to weal at our hands,
still this forms scarcely more than an infinitesimal part of the
demands of the moral law.   The proper end-subject of the
great mass of our moral acts is man.   In this connection we
may view man in three ways—self, other individuals, and society as an organized unit.   Which of these, or in what respect is each of these a true end-subject of the moral law?

Since duty commands man to will the good and he is himself susceptible to weal, his own good must surely fall under
the imperatives of the law.   He is thus himself a true end-
subject of his own moral conduct.   As a large part of the
needs of the individual are provided for by his egoistic impulses, comparatively little is left to the moral law or conscious feeling of duty.   Yet this little is of the highest importance.   It is the sense of duty to self which commands
us often in spite of all egoistic impulses and inclinations, to
seek the highest good, the lasting or the spiritual good, in
place of the lower, temporary, or sensuous goods.   It is self-
respect which enforces the duty of the present self to the
future self and of the lower self to the higher self.   The
sublimity of the moral law and the dignity of character are
manifested quite as clearly in the victory of the higher over

the lower nature in cases concerning the individual himself alone as in the more public examples of the sacrifice of self to the good of others. Our own immediate susceptibility to the higher forms of good is a sufficient justification of duties to ourselves. It seems a forced, circuitous, and altogether superfluous explanation to ground such duties on our relation to society.

Bearing in mind our criterion of susceptibility to weal and the fact that the egoistic impulses are generally pressing us on with a much greater intensity than the sympathetic, we find accordingly the principal end of morality in the welfare of our fellow men. The great majority of our moral imperatives have others as end-subjects. So overwhelmingly large is this portion of the ethical code that it is often thought to include the entire content of the moral law. But as we have already seen, it would seem necessary to reserve to self and even to the lower animals some place within the sacred precincts of Duty's temple.

Now are our duties to others due to them as individuals or as members of society? Only a being who is susceptible to weal, who has the knowledge of good and evil, only a consciousness can be of intrinsic moral worth or be an end-subject of the moral law. The social organism is not a sentient being, a consciousness. It is only its members that possess real consciousness. Society is an interrelated, interacting aggregate of individuals. As far as they have common aims and purposes, they can seek them through society as an organized body. But when we apply the term organism to society we must recognize the essential difference between the social organism and the organism of the human body. Society is susceptible to weal only in its members; the human body not in its members but only as a whole. In the one case the whole is a means, the members the end; in the other the members are the means and the whole is the end. The individual consciousness is the only real human consciousness of which we have any knowledge. Such an expression as the national consciousness may be highly useful as a figure of speech. The personification of the nation or of society is con-

venient in discourse.   But we must not be misled by such a
figure into supposing that the nation is a person with feelings, intellect, and will.   It is only individuals, after all, who
have feelings, who are susceptible to weal.   Only where
there is an autocrat who arrogates to himself to be the state
could there be any meaning in calling the state an end-subject.

Individualism has erred in regarding the single man in a
'state of nature' as complete in himself.   Apart from latent
social capacities and needs such a being would be only an
animal and not worthy of the name man at all.   Indeed the
lone individual is only an abstraction ; we know men only
in society.   Man as man is a social being, ζῶον πολιτικόν,
as Aristotle long ago taught.   It is only in interrelation with
his fellows that the distinctively human qualities are capable
of development at all.   Man is not possessed of innumerable
rights in a state of nature which he agrees willingly or un-
willingly to abrogate in order to enjoy certain social advan-
tages.   It is only in society that he acquires any 'rights' or
rises to a place of moral worth.   Powers and capacities latent
in the natural or isolated man, were there any such, are
actualized in society.   To live is to be in interactive relations,—the broader and deeper the relations the broader
and deeper the life.   For self-realization or living the com-
pletest possible life society is intrinsically necessary.   This
is the truth that has led Wundt and Ihering, conscious of
the defects of the old individualism, to make society the end
and aim of all morality.   Society is not the end-subject.
The individual is the only possible end-subject.   But society
is the absolutely indispensible means for this end.   Man is
in his very nature a social being.   His welfare can be wrought
out only in company with his fellow men.   But ultimately,
after recognizing to the full the unique and indispensable
value of society to mankind, we must say that society exists
for man and not man for society.   Society is the means, individuals are ends.   Only persons susceptible to weal and
capable of character possess intrinsic moral worth.

The discussion of the ends of the moral law, as already

stated, involves not only the question whose good, but also what goods. Besides the end-subjects of the law we must consider the objective ends of the law. These objective ends must correspond to the nature of the end-subjects. In order to determine the content of our duties to self and to others, we have only to inquire: What are the kinds of goods to which man is susceptible? What are the needs of our nature whose satisfaction is necessary that we may attain to the full perfection of our manhood? These needs may be summed up under four general classes : physical, intellectual, æsthetic, and religious. History has already developed for us the formulas and institutions by which we can attain to an approximate satisfaction of these wants. Our primary duty therefore is to obey the moral code and further the institutions established by society. Since this code and these institutions are the product of evolution, we may trust that they will be subject to a still higher development in the future. An important secondary duty, accordingly, is to aid in this development.

§ 17. After what has already been said of the nature and ends of the moral law, little need be added about the motive. For a rational being ends and motives must correspond. We intuitively recognize that the good is worthy to be chosen and that we ought to choose it. This deepest of all realities of our nature, the feeling of moral obligation, is the ultimate motive. This imperative within us calling upon us to choose the good of others before our own, is for the most part justified by our peculiar dependence upon the society of others. That the imperative sometimes overrides the will to live and demands the sacrifice of life itself to others is indeed a moral antinomy. Only the postulate of a future life, in which the individual may continue his self-realization in the society of those other selves whose realization he has aided, seems to offer any solution. That our moral nature should demand of us an absolute self-sacrifice seems impossible to believe.

4

BIBLIOGRAPHY.

Alexander, *Moral Order and Progress.*

Andrews, *Institutes of General History; The Social Body* (in Andover Review, October, 1890).

Aquinas, *Summa Theologica.*

Aristotle, *Ethics ; Rhetoric.*

Bagehot, *Physics and Politics.*

De Coulanges, *The Ancient City.*

Erdmann, *History of Philosophy.*

Eucken, *The Fundamental Concepts of Modern Philosophic Thought.*

Green, *Prolegomena to Ethics.*

Grote, *History of Greece.*

Hobbes, *Leviathan ; Elements of Law.*

Höffding, *Ethik ; Law of· Relativity of Ethics* (in International Journal of Ethics, October, 1890).

Holland, *Elements of Jurisprudence.*

Hume, *Treatise on Human Nature.*

Hunter, *Roman Law.*

Ihering, *Zweck im Recht,* Vol. II.

Jodl, *Geschichte der Ethik.*

Kant, *Grundlegung zur Metaphysik der Sitten ; Kritik der praktischen Vernunft ;* (Abbott's translation of Kant's ethical works).

Locke, *Essay Concerning Human Understanding.*

Maine, *Early History of Institutions; Early Law and Custom ; Ancient Law.*

Morey, *Outlines of Roman Law.*

Muirhead, *Law of Rome.*

Max Müller, *Origin and Growth of Religion.*

Paley, *Principles of Moral and Political Philosophy.*

Robinson, *Principles and Practice of Morality.*

Rümelin, *Reden und Aufsätze : ueber Gesetze der Geschichte, Eine Defenition des Rechts.*

Schmidt, *Die Ethik der Alten Griechen.*

Schurman, *Kantian Ethics and the Ethics of Evolution ; The Ethical Import of Darwinism.*

Sidgwick, *Methods of Ethics ; History of Ethics.*

Stephen, *Science of Ethics.*

Spencer, *Data of Ethics.*

Sophocles, *Antigone.*

Wundt, *Ethik.*

Zeller, *Vorträge und Abhandugen,* 3 *Samml. ueber Begriff und Begründung der Sittlichen Gesetze ; History of Greek Philosophy.*

Ziegler, *Geschichte der Ethik.*